WATCH

BY ASHLEY E. DOWELL

Dowell HOUSE Publishing
WWW.DOWELLHOUSEPUBLISHING.COM

ISBN: 978-1-7362297-0-5 (Hardback)
ISBN: 978-1-7362297-3-6 (Paperback)
ISBN: 978-1-7362297-2-9 (Ebook)

Library of Congress Control Number: 2020951149

Printed in the United States of America.

First printing, 2020.

Dowell House Publishing
Columbus, Ohio
www.dowellhousepublishing.com

For my Soph

"Momma, let's go in. There's nothing here to see."

"Wait, Little One. Watch and you will see a sky that changes beautifully."

Watch and Wait.

"What's that Momma?"

"That's a cloud."

"Why does it move so fast?"

"Sometimes they move fast.
Sometimes they move slow.
It's the wind that moves them so.
We cannot see it but it's there.
Feel it blowing through your hair!"

Watch and *Feel*

"Oh Look! The wind has brought me a leaf!"

"What's that sound, Momma? It's getting very loud.
Listen, Momma! Is that the sound of the clouds?"

"No Dear, clouds make no sound.
This is something new!
We should see it in a few."

Watch and Listen

"A 'copter!"

"Yes, it's a helicopter way up there!
Its wings just chop, chop, **chop** through the air!"

"Nothing now."

"I know but the sky is changing.
The colors will be rearranging."

Watch and *See*

"There's an airplane going up, up, **up!**
Where's it going, Momma?"

"Maybe to  *China* or  *Tennessee.*

Maybe to  *France* or  *Milwaukee.*"

"The sun is going down. Do you see all the colors?"

"Yes, I do!"

"How do they make you feel?"

"They make me feel happy!"

Watch and Feel Happy

"Is that a bird, Momma?"

"It looks like a bird,
but if it's big or small I cannot say.
Let's watch and see where it flies today."

"Wow!   Lots of birds!"

"The sun has almost set and look!
A star!
The star that tells you where you are.
It's the North Star and the first star at night.
Sailors will often follow its light."

Watch and Find

"Here's a bug that I caught in my hand!
Want to see?"

"It's a *firefly* bright as can be!"

"Look up, Darling. The stars are all here! How beautifully they sparkle so.
Let's count some stars and then we can go."

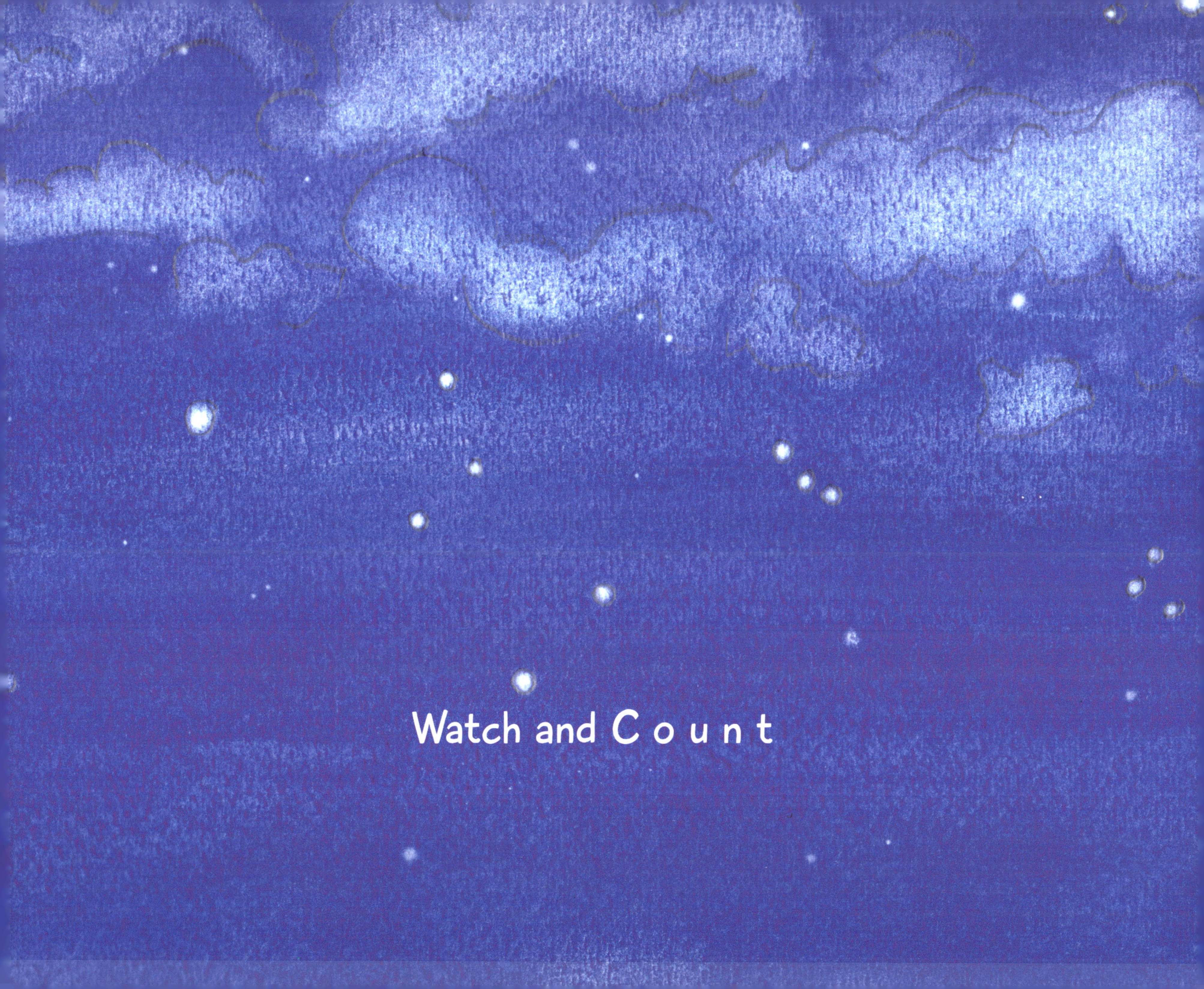

Watch and Count

"It's dark in your room
but when you close
your eyes
think of watching
the moon and
the stars
in the sky."

"Watch all of the clouds
and all of the birds.
Watch me now
and remember
my words."

Watch and Remember...

I love you as high
As the clouds in the sky,
And as hard as
The cold wind can blow.

My love is as bright
As the warm morning light,
And as soft as
The firefly's glow.

My love is much more
Than the birds that can soar,
And as far as
The airplanes can go.

My love will not end.
It will last through the night.
And so calmly you wait
And you know.

Watch and Sleep

www.ingramcontent.com/pod-product-compliance
Lightning Source LLC
Chambersburg PA
CBHW041553030426

42336CB00004B/56